The battle of the supernaturals (monster shower tales)

By:Anthony Hawkins

ISBN:978-1-312-65936-0

Cover Art By Anthony Hawkins

Dedicated to the gay and lesbian community.

Tale # 1:The battle of the supernaturals (monster shower tales)

By:Anthony Hawkins

Dedicated to the gay and lesbian community.

Prologue

It was a dark saturday night,and young handsome 20 year old Zane was sitting at home alone with his equally handsome boyfriend Jarod as they played a hand of cards together at the chairs and table near the center of their living area window.

Chapter 1

I kicked your ass three times in spades man,let's go to sleep now,you wanna play all night and shit,all im going do is keep kicking your ass,Jarod spoke to Zane as Zane snickered in response.Naw,let's go another hand,you scared im going kick your ass this time,Zane spoke back to Jarod as Jarod snickered deeply as if he thought Zane was fooling himself.

Man let's go to sleep man,you aint going beat me,im getting tired,and im kind of horny,Jarod spoke to Zane as Zane sighed in humor and disappointment,Zane wanting to go another hand.Alright,whatever man,we go another hand tomorrow,Zane spoke to Jarod as they both stood from the table.Im about to hop in the shower before i get in the bed,you trying come with me? Jarod spoke to Zane in an almost flirtatious tone.Alright,i wash your back,Zane spoke to Jarod as he and Jarod then began to head to their bathroom down the hall together.

Both Zane and Jarod began to take off their clothes as they entered the bathroom,Zane shrugging out of his fitted boxer briefs as Jarod eyed his round firm buttocks lustfully while taking off his own clothes in the process.

Zane and Jarod stepped into the bathtub together after they were fully naked,their bodies both standing under the showerhead as Jarod began to twist it on,the showerhead then pouring onto them like rain,but hot rain instead.

Zane and Jarod conversed as they stood naked under the showerhead together,their hands soaping their bodies.Both Zane and Jarod then became startled as they heard a creaking sound coming from the living area,slight fear on their faces.You locked the door when you came in today right? Zane questioned Jarod with confusion.Yea i locked the door,you heard that sound out in the living room too? Jarod spoke to Zane.Yea i did,i thought i was going crazy at first,Zane spoke back to Jarod.

Jarod and Zane rinsed themselves off and then silently stepped out of the bathtub as they dried themselves with clean white short above knee length towels and then wrapped them around the waists of their smooth toned naked bodies,and then stepping their feet into shower shoes as they crept out of the bathroom and into the living area together silently.

Yea,told you i was going come for you nigga,a man spoke to Zane as Zane and Jarod came into full view of him in only but the short towels around their waists,Zane watching the man with confused and fearful eyes.Dude what is you doing here man,you came all the way over here because of some shit we was beefing over on facebook? Zane spoke to the man.You sick in the head man,i dont like that shit you be writing on your wall,i dont wanna hear about that faggot shit,the man spoke to Zane,the man dressed in a hat and a fitted tank top,his skin just as smoothly brown as Zane and Jarod's,tho Zane and Jarod's smooth brown skin had a subtle radiance.

Talk that shit you was saying online now punk,the man spoke to

Zane.Dude you started it with me first dude,you came on my page posting shit about how i needed to stop posting this and that,then after i told you to chill you was still coming at me sideways,dude i dont even know your real name like that,your name Ceddy_2011 online right? Zane spoke to the man as if he were trying to calm him.

Yea,thats my name,but check this too,the man known as Ceddy_2011 pulled a gun from his pants pocket to aim it directly at Zane.Dude chill man,you getting hyped over some facebook and online shit tho?! Jarod spoke angrily to Ceddy_2011 as Ceddy_2011 ignored him.Im going pop you and your faggot ass boyfriend,sick ass niggas man,that gay shit is wrong dawg,Ceddy_2011 cocked his gun as he prepared to fire at Zane and Jarod both.

Dude let's talk this out,this aint gotta be taken there man,Zane spoke to Ceddy_2011,tho Ceddy_2011 didn't want to see reason,he just wanted to hurt Zane in anyway he could.Ceddy_2011 then fired one round off at Zane without a word as Zane saw the bullet approaching him with precise vision moving slower than himself,Zane dodging the bullet quickly as he disappeared from Ceddy_2011's sight in a near blur of quick speed.

Ceddy_2011 looked all around the room for Zane's whereabouts,but soon felt his arm being pulled violently behind his back in a snapping painful sound of his breaking bones.Ceddy_2011 turned to see that it was Zane behind him as he yelled out in pain of his arm being broken.He a vampire man,i can smell it on him Zane,it was more to why he aint like you,he dont like you because you a werewolf man,his kind had us in slavery at one point in time,they mad they cant control us no more,they think they can tell the whole world what to do,the human world,and the supernatural world,this nigga just fed and killed too,i smell blood on him,human blood,Jarod spoke to Zane as Zane continued to restrain Ceddy_2011 roughly.

Im going kill yall two sick ass niggas! Ceddy_2011 screamed loudly at the top of his lungs as his eyes turned a blood red color,his face insane with bloodlust and pure hatred for Zane and Jarod.We gotta take this nigga out man,he going go back and bring more of his kind if we let him go,dudes like him aint going stop attacking us until we dead Zane,we gotta handle him right here and now,Jarod spoke sternly to Zane.Ceddy_2011 turned to attack Zane with his other free and unbroken arm,but had it caught by Zane's fast and strong grip,Zane then squeezing his nails into the flesh of Ceddy_2011's arm as he began to twist it out of place in a crunching sound of Ceddy_2011's breaking bones as Ceddy_2011 yelled out in deep pain.

Jarod then began to transform into a wolflike humanoid as his body grew in size,the towel around the waist of his naked body falling from his waist to the floor in a light thump as his new size and muscled strength extended and inflated from out of it,a powerful and immense roar then releasing from Jarod's throat as his transformation was complete.

Jarod's new wolflike body stood very tall and strong,his huge sex organs covered with thick fur,tho they were still visible somewhat,fur tracing down his chest to his navel and then his crotch area,sharp canines sprouting from his gums,his hands having claws.

Ceddy_2011 turned to meet Jarod in wolflike form but then had the entire left side of his face torn off by Jarod's sharp canines in a bloody scream of his own lips,blood rushing from out of the exposed muscle and tissue of his wounded face as Jarod then pushed his claws through his chest as Zane saw the claws come out the other side.Ceddy_2011 began to choke out in pain and near death as Jarod twisted his claws around even further into his open wounded chest,and then swiftly pulling them out leaving a huge hole in the middle of Ceddy_2011's stomach,Ceddy_2011's internal organs obliterated by Jarod's claws as his broken arms sagged from his shoulders as Zane let him go from his grip.

Ceddy_2011 began to shout insults at Zane and Jarod but then abruptly had his head ripped off by Zane's very own hands as Zane twisted it off in a crunchy wet and bloody sound as blood oozed out from Ceddy_2011's detached head,Ceddy_2011's headless bloody body then drooping and falling to the floor in a thump as blood poured from it's headless stump.

Man we gotta dismember this dude fully or he might heal,Jarod quickly spoke to Zane as Zane held

Ceddy_2011's severed head in his fingers tightly.

Chapter 2

Zane studied Ceddy_2011's detached head with disgust as it swung from his fingers,blood dripping from the torn stump of it where the neck was once attached.Zane then flung Ceddy_2011's severed head onto the hardwood floor in a nonchalant manner as both he and Jarod then studied Ceddy_2011's headless body that laid before their feet,Jarod's huge wolflike body snarling above angrily as his canines that were covered in Ceddy_2011's blood showed.

Jarod gave Zane a silent signal as he looked over to Zane,Zane then beginning to transform into a huge wolflike humanoid himself as his towel fell from his naked waist,his body then standing naked and slightly covered with thin fur in certain areas just as Jarod did.Zane and Jarod didn't communicate with words once they were wolflike beings,but through signals,signals only they understood.

Both Zane and Jarod looked down at Ceddy_2011's limp and still slightly moving body as they then quickly and ferociously got down on all fours to feast on his wounded body fiercely with the tearing of Ceddy_2011's flesh echoing throughout the house,their strong jaws and canines clamping down heavily each time they tore ribbons of flesh from Ceddy_2011's body,blood soaking their snouts and teeth and the floor they feasted upon.

Jarod and Zane didn't eat or swallow Ceddy_2011's body in consumption,but rather tore him limb from limb until he was scattered all across the room in many pieces,his arms here,and his legs there,and his torso over there,some torn flesh peeled from his body in the process.

Both Zane and Jarod finally stood to their hind legs again as they began to revert back into their human forms again,their bodies standing naked and covered in Ceddy_2011's blood as they watched his remains scattered all around the room in bloody chunks.

We gotta burn this nigga now man,hurry up,we gotta get up every piece,Jarod spoke to Zane as he and Zane quickly began to toss Ceddy_2011's remains into a black plastic bag,placing his severed head in last,and then tying the bag tightly as they both headed towards the front door that was slightly opened from Ceddy_2011's previous break in before his brutal attack by Zane and

Jarod that left him bloodily dismembered and mutilated.

Zane peeped out of the front door to check for passing civilians,but the night was dark and quiet and empty,the woods just across the street,Zane and Jarod's neighborhood having few residents and being very secluded somewhat.

Zane and Jarod didn't bother to get dressed as they both headed out into the woods in their nudity to burn Ceddy_2011's remains.Zane and

Jarod didn't stop moving until they were far and deep into the woods where no one would see the fire they were planning to ignite.

Jarod morphed into his wolflike form and then began to dig into the soil deep,ripping up grass and dirt in the process as a dog would when they were trying to escape a fence,Ceddy_2011's bag of remains resting inbetween Zane's fingers.Alright,here we go,this deep enough,Jarod spoke to Zane as he reverted into his human form and stood up again,dirt covering his once clawed hands.

Zane tossed Ceddy_2011's bag of remains into the dug up dirt pit,and then lit it with a lighter he carried in his free hand after Jarod drenched the remains with gasoline,the flames brilliantly rising upwards giving off heat and light as both Zane and Jarod watched Ceddy_2011's bag of remains burn and scorch,the fire soon consuming the plastic bag and partly the remains in fumes of cooking flesh and plastic.

Let's get out this joint man,i dont wanna keep watching this shit,Zane spoke to Jarod as they both turned to head back home after giving Ceddy_2011 a fiery grave.

Chapter 3

Zane and Jarod headed into the house after torching Ceddy_2011's dead remains and then began to clean their house of all of Ceddy_2011's blood that was splattered all over their hardwood floor,their nude bodies still covered with the deceased Ceddy_2011's blood.

Zane and Jarod soon headed into the bathroom to shower and clean themselves of Ceddy_2011's blood as they both showered together under the hot raining showerhead with soap,suds running down their naked bodies as they kissed lightly here and there on the lips.

Zane and Jarod headed out of the shower clean and naked as they placed short white above knee length towels around the waists of their naked toned bodies,their feet sliding into shower shoes as they both entered into the living area together side by side.

Jarod gave Zane a smooth and long kiss on the lips as they headed into their bedroom,their bodies standing naked flesh to naked flesh,chest to chest,towel to towel,thigh to thigh,knee to knee,foot to foot in passion as Jarod then eased their door shut to proceed with their passion and romance.

Jarod and Zane began to touch all over each other as they both eased themselves to their shared bed in lust,their lustful and very passion filled kisses giving off smooching sounds of the smooth flesh of their lips as their hands groped each other intimately.Jarod soon unwrapped the towel from around the waist of his naked body and then slid Zane's towel off of his naked body as well,their nakedness now meeting just as their lips did,their loins throbbing in lust.

Jarod and Zane soon connected flesh to flesh as Jarod eased his erect and rock hard penis up inside and inbetween Zane's tight fleshly walls as both he and Zane moaned out in pleasure of their flesh meeting.Jarod then began to move himself up and down on Zane as their bodies sexually collided in their hot nudity,the bed squeaking a bit as they both moaned out in lust and intense pleasure.

Jarod's exposed buttocks flexed and rotated back and forth as he made deep and passionate love to Zane on the bed,his naked body bumping and shoveling onto and into Zane's own naked body in fleshly pleasure as both their loins began to insanely heat up in ecstasy.Jarod then began to speed up he and Zane's love making,Jarod shoveling himself deeply into Zane as a dog in heat would,his buttocks twitching and flexing swiftly in the pleasurable process as he and Zane heavily moaned out in their naked fleshly pleasure.

Jarod felt his huge and thick penis throbbing and filling with hot semen from his thick round plump testicle sack as he continued to stab up inside Zane in long smooth strokes,Zane's inner fleshly walls pulsing and being pricked from the inside with Jarod's heavy penis in pleasure points of inner nerves.

Jarod's naked body bounced up and down on top of Zane's naked body in a tight flesh connection of their bodies a few more times until Zane was entering sexual completion,Jarod then swiftly snatching his penis out of Zane as it swelled with semen and then began to ejaculate all over Zane's toned smooth naked body in intense throbbing pleasure as Zane erupted with a hot orgasm of his own,their naked mating reaching a climax of sexaul satisfaction and completion.

Jarod's penis shot long thick streams of hot semen all over Zane's naked smooth abs as Jarod then massaged the wetness of his hot semen all around Zane's nude body and crotch with the plump mushroom shaped tip of his thick heavy penis as his own nude body flexed in jerking pleasure,Jarod then laying himself on top of Zane as Zane held him in his arms,Zane's fingers tracing up and down along Jarod's smooth exposed back and buttocks as they both laid naked in hot perspiration on their bed in sexual gratification and passion and silence for hours.

Chapter 4

Zane and Jarod wiped themselves down with soaked hand cloths and then placed their towels back around the naked waists of their bodies as they headed back out into their living area closely side by side as their shower shoes thumped along the hardwood floor.

In a quick flash Zane's body was hurled away from along Jarod's side as he was pulled up the wall by an invisible force as Jarod watched in worry and concern and fear for him,Jarod trying to help Zane,but not being able to move from the spot he stood,as if he were glued to the floor by something invisible as well.

That bloodsucker Ced told me werewolves were in this town,but i thought he was lying to get me to come here so he could set a trap for me,i would've killed him too,but you two already did that for me,i found his burning corpse after i scried for him,a woman spoke to both Zane and Jarod as she held out both her hands,her hands seeming as if they were controlling Zane and Jarod's movements invisibly,and they were.

Fucking witch,let my dude Zane go! Jarod spoke to the woman through his teeth as he tried to move,but couldn't.It's nothing personal,but i cant keep yall alive,yall a threat to my coven and people,only one species can survive,werewolves and vampires,and other species give too much attention to all of our supernatural world,newly turned werewolves and vampires attack people like crazy,when the dead body numbers start rising humans start talking,witches are more in tuned with nature,your kind is freaks of nature,the supernatural powered woman spoke to Zane and Jarod with conviction.

Man werewolves and vampires are only dangerous if they already evil when they was human,both the werewolf gene and the vampire virus only heightens whats already in you,i turned and created Zane through sexual intercourse when we met at a gay bathhouse and i helped him with it,werewolves might lose a bit of their humanity when they first turn but they get it back a hour later once they gain control of their wolf,same with vampires,all of them aint bad,some of them just let their thirst for blood control them when they first get turned,and some just like killing motherfuckers,all witches aint innocent either,so many of yall then put hexes on niggas and killed people that regular humans sometimes call unexplainable deaths,Jarod spoke to the woman.

I understand,but i cant let yall live,the woman spoke to Jarod as she pulled Zane up against the wall further with her invisible grip of magic of the sort,Zane unable to flinch,but just a little,the flesh of his exposed back tightly pressing against the wall as his naked towel covered buttocks did as well,his legs and arms dangeling as he sat up on the ceiling still being held in an invisible grip by the woman.

I prepared a special blade that would paralyze yall forever since i cant kill you two by other means,i know how yall kind heals fast if not killed in the right way,i blessed this blade,me and some of my sister witches and brothers did,some other witch covens and tribes too,we wanted to make sure this worked on specific supernatural groups,we couldn't take a chance,the woman spoke to Jarod and Zane as she pulled a sharp blade from her pants pocket,the blade looking as if it were dipped in silver nitrate.

The woman approached Jarod with the blade as Jarod tried to move,and then quickly swiped the blade across Jarod's forearm without penetrating the skin as the silver nitrate began to slither from the blade and then all the way up Jarod's forearm and body until it completely coated his naked body in a hardening silver nitrate encase,leaving Jarod paralyzed and frozen solid in place,his towel around his naked waist and the shower shoes on his feet the only thing not frozen in silver nitrate as the rest of his body looked like a living statue of a practically naked man.

Zane yelled in anger as he watched Jarod be turned into a naked living towel covered statue before his very eyes below,his anger swelling him into his huge wolflike humanoid form as his naked body inflated out of his towel violently while his towel then fell to the hardwood floor below him,his powerful wolflike form enabling him to break free of the woman's magic with his raw increased strength of being both man and beast.

The woman tried her best to keep Zane from fully escaping her grip but failed as Zane broke free and fell from the ceiling landing on his feet like a cat,his enraged eyes and growling snout watching the woman angrily for what she had done to Jarod as the woman flinched back in slight fear.

The woman then dropped her blade onto the floor as she conjured it into a black python looking snake that began to slither towards Zane,the snake making hissing sounds as it's body slithered it's way to Zane.

Zane headed to the snake boldly and then fell on all fours purposely as he began to murmur low snarls at the snake as the snake stop to listen as if it were being enchanted by a snake charmer,Zane's wolf form being able to communicate with other animals,and manipulate them through pheromones through his pores.

The snake then sat it's body upwards and then turned towards the woman,and then quickly heading back to her in a quick slither of it's body to attack her instead,the woman trying to stop it,but the magic from the blade it was conjured being too strong for her to control and overpower.

The snake coiled itself around the woman and then began to enter into her mouth forcefully as it slithered down her throat while she gagged and choked in extreme discomfort,the snake then biting her from the inside with it's silver nitrate venom covered fangs.

The woman began to shake violently and uncontrollably as her shaking slowed down as she began to fall into paralyzation and then encasing in hardening silver nitrate as her body was then completely coated in hard silver nitrate except for her clothes still on her body,her body now a living statue just as Jarod was.

Zane headed over to Jarod with tear filled eyes as he watched Jarod's body still and frozen in hard silver,but soon Jarod's body beginning to thaw as the silver began to cook and crack from his intense body heat as Zane watched him with amazement and hope,Jarod's flesh showing through the cracks.

The silver then completely shattered and fell and crumbled from Jarod's

body as his smooth bare brown skin
was no longer coated with silver
nitrate,both he and Zane then
hugging swiftly in a deep emotional
embrace.

Both Jarod and Zane then looked
over to the woman as she was frozen
solid in silver,Jarod then heading
towards her as he then strongly
kicked her,the shower shoes on his
bare feet making thunderous impact
on her cracking body from Jarod's
strength as she then fully cracked and
fell to pieces on the floor an unliving
broken statue.

Jarod then scooped the broken and shattered witch woman's crumbled body pieces up by her clothes as most was still inside,and then took her out to the trashcan where he left her crumbled and shattered like shards of glass in a bag.

Jarod headed back inside with Zane and then shut and locked the front door behind him as he and Zane stared at each other silently and then began kissing passionately in relief they were in each others arms again safe.

Zane and Jarod decided to take a run through the woods as they headed outside in blurry quick speed of their supernatural werewolf abilities,their bodies bolting through the woods alongside each other in only the short white towels around the waists of their naked bodies in hyper speed until they stopped along a cliff where they both positioned themselves and howled side by side as mates to the moon in the dark night as they both transformed into their werewolf forms as their towels dropped to the grass below them from their strong nude bodies.

The end

Tale # 2:(Pack Brothas Shower)

By:Anthony Hawkins

Dedicated to the gay and lesbian community.

Prologue

It was a dark night in the town of Forest Lake Terrace,and tho the sun wasn't out the air was still hot and moist.Forest Lake Terrace was a quiet town in the countrysides,with few residents,only a few houses on each piece of owned land.Some of the residents lived far out in the woods,like Andre and his brother Dorian,and their father Deandre.

Deandre raised his two sons Andre and Dorian together in a huge mansion like house,a house with six bedrooms,a private bathroom in each room and one public bathroom,a grand hall and a huge master bath.Tho Deandre raised both young men as his own,Dorian wasn't his biological son,but Andre was.

Deandre had found Dorian in the woods outside of town,abandoned and alone,and just a baby.Deandre took Dorian in,giving him the name Dorian,since the name Dorian began with a D like his.Deandre did the same with his own son Andre,just shaving off a few letters,and calling him Andre,similar to

Deandre.Deandre was a decent wealthy and educated man,but he wasn't just a man,but a shapeshifter,a person who could change from man to beast.

Deandre's two sons Andre and Dorian were shapeshifters as well,Andre inheriting his shapeshifter gene from Deandre,and Dorian inheriting his from another shapeshifter pack,an unknown pack.

Shapeshifters were able to sense and smell one another,Just as they could with humans,which is how Deandre found Dorian in the first place.Andre and Dorian both were now in their

20's,and still kicking it with their father Deandre,who hadn't aged a bit,still looking as if he was in his early 30's or late 20's,because shapshifters didn't age.

Tho Deandre left the house to Andre and Dorian,he still visited them from time to time,checking in on them.Andre and Dorian had grown into handsome and sexy young men,Andre being around six feet tall with smooth dark brown chocolate colored skin and full lips that had a peachy tone to the bottom,and facial hair that was neatly trimmed around his kissable lips into a sharp goatee,teeth as white as snow,and long dark hair that he wore in a thick ponytail.Andre had a sculpted and muscular physique,abs that showed visibly,and pecks that bulged,and thighs that could crush boulders,and muscles that were touchable but not overbearing,and an ass that could hold up a wineglass,with a ten inch dick to go with it.

Dorian was equally as attractive as Andre,having a similar sculpted and muscular physique like Andre,but with silky light golden brown skin just two or three shades lighter than Andre's and a thinner straight goatee

around his soft and full lips.Dorian
had dark hair as well,tho his hair was
cut short in a neat fade and slightly
more wavy in detail,but thick
too.Dorian stood around the same
height as Andre,and their father
Deandre stood slightly taller than
them both.

Tho Andre,Dorian and Deandre all
had their own personalities,they all
had a few things in common,and one
of those things was the fact that they
were all gay,and african american,tho
Dorian slightly looked as if he had
traces of latino in him as well.

Chapter 1

The night was still young,and Andre and Dorian were ready to have a good time,inviting three guys over to their house,in hopes of having a night of good sex.

Dude in the silk shirt is mine dawg,Dorian smirked at Andre as they both watched the three guys they called over pull up in a silver volvo.They all sexy as hell,so i dont care,but dude in the black jeans looking good over there,Andre smirked back at Dorian,his eyes watching the men step onto their stone pathway.Dorian opened the front door as the three young men approached.

Ay,what's up yall,what's good?! Dorian questioned the men as they made their way to the front door,stopping.We cool,we came over because we trying freak,what's good wit chall? One of the men smiled thinly at Dorian and Andre.That's what's up,come on in,Andre invited the three guys in.

Andre wore a black tank top with a pair of black denim jeans,while

Dorian wore a white tank top with a pair of blue denim jeans.Where can i put this? One of the guys asked Andre as he took off his coat.You can put it on that coat rack over there,Andre explained to the man,pointing his finger to the coat rack a few feet away from the front door.

Cool,the man spoke to Andre as he headed over to the coat rack,placing his coat on it.Im trying fuck,on the real,another guy spoke to Dorian and Andre,becoming impatient.Alright,so what's yall names and shit? Dorian questioned the three guys.

My name Winston,make sure yall remember that,my sex is on point,Winston spoke to Andre and Dorian,his eyes watching their faces.Nigga take the shades off,can we see ya eyes dawg? Dorian smiled at Winston.No problem my man,Winston spoke to Dorian as he took off his shades.

My name Vince,im smooth and i can lay that pipe,that's all yall need to know,Vince spoke smoothly to Dorian and Andre,biting down on his lip a little.Vince was the cocky type.

Im Richy,people call me Ric tho,Richy introduced himself to Andre and

Dorian,a sexy but arrogant smile on his face.Alright cool,im Andre and this my brother Dorian,not by blood tho,Andre introduced himself and Dorian to Winston,Vince and Richy.

So yall trying get busy or what? Vince spoke to everyone in the room.Come chill wit me upstairs in my room,Dorian spoke to Vince,giving Vince a quick nodd of his head.Dorian and Vince headed up the stairs as Andre and the others stayed downstairs.

What chall trying get into? Andre spoke to Winston and Richy.It's whatever,let's go in ya room,Winston spoke to Andre.Shid,im down for anything,im horny as fuck,Richy explained to Andre and Winston.Alright,cool,let's go to one of the lower rooms tho,Andre spoke to Winston and Richy as he turned the other way and then began to head to one of the bedrooms.

Chapter 2

Andre only brought guys he was feeling on a deep level into his bedroom,never quick flings.Andre took Winston and Richy into a big bedroom at the far edge of the house,and then shut the door behind them.

Im not trying get in ya business or nothing,but do you and ya brother fuck sometimes? Richy spoke to Andre,his eyes on Andre's face.Hell naw,that's my homeboy,my bro,we aint never did nothing like that,Andre explained to Richy,chuckling slightly.

Nigga yall some lames,if i had a brother that looked like you or ya brother i would have been smashed one of ya'll,on the real,it's not like yall blood related,shid,Richy smirked at

Andre.Dude you wild,Andre smiled thinly at Richy.Yall niggas talking and shit,and im sitting here ready to get down,Winston explained to Andre and Richy.

Winston shrugged out of his shirt and then pulled himself closer to Andre as he and Andre's lips got closer.Richy was about to take off something too,until he heard a loud voice outside the bedroom door.

Andre,come here right quick bro,it's some family business! Dorian spoke outside the bedroom door.What happened,everything cool? Andre questioned Dorian with worry as he flung open the bedroom door.Naw man,i gotta speak wit chu in private man,shit is crazy,Dorian spoke to Andre,pulling Andre to the side.

Man i almost changed in front of that dude upstairs dawg,Dorian whispered to Andre as Andre listened.You what,how? Andre questioned Dorian silently with concern in his face.Hell yea man,i could feel my muscles spasm and shit dawg,Dorian explained quietly to Andre.

Oh shit,we forgot it was a full moon tonight,Andre spoke to Dorian,realizing what caused Dorian to suddenly change without wanting to make the change.Alright,let's get rid of these dudes,and then we going hit the woods man,Andre explained very quietly to Dorian as Vince headed slowly back down the stairs,his face confused.

Why you just leave me like that dawg? Vince questioned Dorian as he buttoned up his shirt again.Andre's muscles began to spasm just as Dorian's did,he could feel the change wanting to happen without his consent.

Ay yall,maybe we can do this some other time,we bout to take care of some family business right quick,Dorian explained to Vince,Winston and Richy.Yall dudes trippin,yea,we can do this another time but we out for now,peace,Vince spoke to Dorian and Andre,him and Winston and Richy leaving out the house,shutting the door behind them.

Dorian locked the front door behind Vince and the other guys,and then headed back to Andre.Man we just had to invite some dudes over on the night of the full moon,the time when we got problems controlling ourselves and shit,we wasn't even thinking,Dorian spoke to Andre,snickering afterwards.

Shapeshifters changed automatically during the full moon,tho some were able to control it,mostly pure born Shapeshifters like Andre and Dorian,and Deandre,Shapeshifters that were born with the shapeshifter gene,instead of being turned by one.

What the hell you doing? Andre questioned Dorian,seeing him taking off his shirt.Nigga im about to take a shower,you coming? Dorian spoke to Andre,his eyes on Andre's face.Naw,imma go and lay my ass down somewhere,Andre explained to Dorian with a thin smile.

Nigga come on,then we can go hunting in the woods afterwards,just me and you,like we always do,Dorian spoke to Andre,his muscles flexing just a bit.Alright,im coming wit chu,Andre smiled thinly at Dorian.

Brothas for life man,Dorian spoke to Andre as they headed down the big hall of the house into the master bath.Andre and Dorian began shrugging out of all of their clothes,both of them now standing fully naked.Dorian turned on a showerhead,and then got under it.

Come over here man,we can share this one,Dorian explained to Andre,seeing Andre about to turn on the showerhead next to the one he was using.Alright cool,Andre spoke as he headed under the raining showerhead with Dorian.

So what's up,you got it in wit any of them dudes that was here? Dorian questioned Andre with a grin.Naw,we aint really get to do shit,Andre grinned back at Dorian.Shid,i was about to suck dude off,and then let him suck me off,but i started changing and shit dawg,Dorian smiled at Andre as he began soaping himself.I know,i was about to get it popping with both them dudes man,Andre smirked at Dorian as Dorian smirked back.I feel you,im still horny as fuck,Dorian explained to Andre.You aint the only one dude,Andre spoke to Dorian,soap and water pouring down his body.

Nigga if i wasn't ya brotha would you try and holla at me,keep it real dawg,would you? Dorian spoke to Andre,waiting for Andre to reply.Nigga what kind of question is that? Andre snickered at Dorian.

Just a question,now answer it dawg,would you try to holla at me?

Dorian spoke to Andre again,his eyes watching Andre's face.Alright,since you asking me that,would you try and holla at me nigga? Andre spoke to Dorian.Hell yea,nigga you got a good package,i'd suck you and fuck you all motherfucking day,Dorian explained to Andre with a burst of laughter.Eww nigga,Andre laughed deeply at Dorian.Imma keep it real,i would smash you,Andre spoke truthfully to Dorian.There we go,keep that shit a hundred,Dorian smiled thinly at Andre,now letting the hot water beat against his face.

You got buns nigga,Dorian squeezed Andre on the ass,snickering afterwards.Alright nigga,take this,Andre splashed a handful of water on Dorian.Back at chu nigga! Dorian splashed water on Andre as well.

Come here nigga! Andre spoke to Dorian as he grabbed him,both of them play wrestling under the pouring showerhead.Andre got Dorian in a submissive position,Dorian's back to his chest.Now what dawg? Andre spoke to Dorian,still holding him in his grip.Get cha dick off my ass nigga,Dorian joked with Andre,feeling Andre's penis pressing against his wet butt cheeks.

This how the male animals be having the female animals,Andre explained to Dorian as he gently pressed his mouth to the back of Dorian's neck.Andre and Dorian both became silent for awhile,Dorian's back still to Andre's chest.

Andre let Dorian out of his grip and then closed his eyes as he let the water from the showerhead rain down on his face,Dorian doing the same.Andre and Dorian began to speak again,staying in the shower for another half hour,letting the hot water run down their naked bodies.Let's get out this joint now,Dorian spoke to Andre,turning off the showerhead in the process.

Chapter 3

Andre and Dorian pulled short white towels around the waists of their naked bodies,sliding their feet into shower shoes as they exited the master bath.Andre's hair swung over his strong left shoulder as he turned Dorian's way.

Dorian examined Andre's body,starting with Andre's handsome face,and then moving down to Andre's smooth and bulging pecks,and then andre's strong arms,and then Andre's smooth abs,and then Andre's toned and hard thighs and legs that protruded from his short skimpy towel.

Andre watched Dorian's body as well,eyeing Dorian's biceps,and then Dorian's smooth and toned abs,and then Dorian's toned legs and calves that hung from his towel as well.

Both Andre and Dorian's skin glistened just a bit,having a radiance to it's smooth touch.Nigga you looking good over there,Dorian complimented Andre,his eyes still on Andre's body.You looking good too,we aint seen each other like this in a minute,Andre spoke to Dorian.

Let's go watch some porn together,shid,we can jack our dicks together,make it a family thing,Dorian explained to Andre as he moved closer to him.That's cool,Andre Spoke to Dorian,a smile on his face.Sometimes homeys can take care of each other,im ya bro,let

me do you,and you do me,im for real
dude,Dorian explained softly and
quietly to Andre in his smooth and
deep voice.What chu mean by that?
Andre questioned Dorian,already
knowing what Dorian meant,but just
wanting Dorian to confirm it.

You know what i mean nigga,i jerk
your stuff and you jerk mines,some
homeboys do that shit all the
time,personally,i think the shit is
harmless and innocent,Dorian
explained to Andre as Andre listened.

Alright,Andre said swiftly and
smoothly to Dorian,accepting
Dorian's offer for them to masturbate

together to gay adult films.My dick bigger than yours nigga,Dorian spoke to Andre,chuckling afterwards.Nigga please,you wish dawg,Andre spoke back to Dorian,chuckling along with him.Let's measure them then nigga,Dorian spoke to Andre.Alright,that's a bet,Andre spoke quickly to Dorian.

Andre and Dorian moved closer to each other,and then stood side by side,pulling their penises from under their towels into full view,placing them alongside each other,one a bit darker than the other.

We about the same size nigga,so i think it's a tie,Andre smirked at Dorian.whatever dawg,but hold up,watch how this shit feel,Dorian spoke to Andre,smoothly and slowly stroking and grazing he and Andre's penises together in his hand.

Dorian began to stroke he and Andre's penises together even harder and faster as both their penises became erect from the stroking action.

Alright,alright,quit nigga,imma about to bust dawg! Andre stopped Dorian,not wanting to explode his semen in Dorian's hand.Nigga you would've had a handful of nut dawg,if you kept doing that shit,Andre warned Dorian.

Nigga we brothers,we can help each other out every now and then,Dorian spoke to Andre,pulling his hand around Andre's hard penis again.Nigga go ahead,quit dude,Andre moaned to Dorian,telling him to stop,but not really wanting him to.

Dorian ignored Andre's words as he continued to violently but smoothly Jerk and stroke Andre's dick,not caring if Andre told him to stop,because he knew deep down Andre liked it.

Dorian moved his lips closer to Andre's as he continued to savagely beat and jerk Andre's dick even harder,letting the tip of Andre's dick massage into his grip from time to time.

Tho Dorian's lips were close to Andre's they didn't kiss.Dorian watched Andre's facial expressions as he continued to jerk him back and forth in a rhythm,Dorian getting off knowing that he was getting Andre off.

Dorian got to his knees and then threw Andre's hard dick into his mouth,taking it back out to tease the mushroom shaped head of it,and then shoving it back into his warm and wet mouth.This nasty man,Andre moaned out to Dorian,feeling the wetness of Dorian's mouth move smoothly up and down on his hard dick.

Let it be nasty then nigga,Dorian spoke in a muffled voice,gulping Andre's dick sloppily into his warm mouth.Ah,damn dude! Andre moaned out in pleasure,looking down at Dorian,watching Dorian's head bob up and down on his throbbing dick.

Brothers take care of each other nigga,Dorian moaned to Andre,making eye contact with Andre just for a second as he kept sucking Andre's dick,not stopping.

Dorian stroked himself from under his towel as he continued to deep throat Andre's dick from under Andre's towel.Nigga stop dawg,i feel like imma about to bust nigga! Andre warned Dorian as Dorian continued to devour him.Blow that load in my mouth nigga,i dont care,Dorian explained to Andre,tossing Andre's dick back in his mouth,gulping it with his mouth and jerking it with his free hand,wanting a taste of Andre's semen.

Andre hissed in ecstasy as Dorian continued to slurp him.Andre reached his hand behind Dorian,grabbing and squeezing Dorian's tight ass.Damn bro,can i get some of this? Andre spoke to Dorian in a deep heavy breathing voice as his fingers groped Dorian's ass.No problem my brotha,give me that big dick nigga,Dorian whispered to Andre as he stood to his feet again,turning around and then bending over.

Fuck my ass nigga,Dorian ordered Andre,waiting eagerly for Andre to enter into him.Andre pulled Dorian's towel from his waist,letting it drop to the marble floor,and then pulling off the towel around his waist as well,letting his fall beside Dorian's,both he and Dorian now naked.

Andre's plump ass flexed ass he positioned himself near Dorian.Andre examined Dorian's round and protruding ass with deep lust as Dorian pushed it further into the air.Andre wanted to feel his dick deep up in Dorian's ass.

Andre wet his right hand with his tongue and then massaged and lubricated his dick with that same hand.Andre pointed his dick towards the entrance of Dorian's ass,and then smoothly plugged it up into Dorian as Dorian gasped slightly.

Joint is tight man,shit,that's what's up,Andre moaned and complimented Dorian,feeling Dorian's inner muscles squeeze tightly to his hard dick.Andre began to push his dick deeper into Dorian,smoothly plunging it back and forth into Dorian as he held onto Dorian's shoulder,forcing Dorian even further on it.Dorian's ass clapped on

Andre's dick as Andre pounded him hard and smooth.Andre's dick molded to Dorian's hole,as a plug would to a socket.

Andre and Dorian felt connected to each other on a physical and emotional level,and that made their sex even better.

This ass was made for me nigga,Andre moaned to Dorian as he continued to thrust back and forth inside him,hitting corners and angles.Dorian could feel Andre's rod fitted inside his cavity,he could feel Andre's rod excite nerves inside him as he moaned in the pleasure of it all.Show me it was made for me nigga,give me that cum nigga! Dorian spoke to Andre,feeling Andre fucking him hard from behind.

Dorian's hand gripped onto Andre's muscular thigh as Andre pounded him and pounded him,Andre's balls slapping against Dorian,making a sound throughout the room,a sound that was mixed with Dorian and Andre's moans.Andre pushed himself deeper into Dorian as he laid his broad and bare chest to Dorian's bare back,his lips pressing against the side of Dorian's neck.You want all that nut up in that tight ass nigga,Andre moaned to Dorian,fucking him faster.Fuck yea,Dorian spoke to Andre,backing his ass harder and further onto Andre's throbbing and pulsing dick.

Ah,fuck yea man! Andre shouted out in a deep moan of lust and sexual gratification,shooting his hot semen deep into Dorian's round naked ass.Damn man,that shit is nice and hot nigga! Dorian explained to Andre,feeling Andre's semen flood into his cavity as he began shooting off semen of his own in a deep moan of sexual peek and satisfaction.

Andre pulled himself out of Dorian,and then began slapping and grazing Dorian's ass cheeks with his still erect penis,rubbing the excess cum all around and inbetween Dorian's ass.Dorian stood up again,as Andre's now softening dark penis fell from inbetween his ass.Andre hissed and moaned as he watched Dorian's wet ass flex just a bit as Dorian turned towards him.

Shit was hott man,we should do this shit more often bro,fuck them niggas we called over here earlier,Dorian moaned in pleasure to Andre.fuck yea dude,Andre cosigned

Dorian,pulling Dorian closer to him as he rushed his lips into Dorian's,kissing Dorian passionately and lustfully.

Andre and Dorian pressed their foreheads together gently after they finished kissing,calm silence filling the room.

Chapter 4

Andre and Dorian cleaned themselves up from all the sex they had,and then headed out into the woods fully dressed.Im hunting big game today dawg,imma catch like five or six deers nigga,Dorian boasted to Andre.Nigga you go right ahead,imma just watch you,i dont see how you can drain the blood of a damn deer? The shit creeps me out,Andre spoke to Dorian.

Naw,once you taste deer blood in ya panther form the shit not that bad,but once you turn back into human form that shit leave a bad taste in ya mouth,Dorian explained to Andre.Whatever nigga,you ready? Andre spoke to Dorian.I been ready bro,Dorian explained to Andre.

Andre and Dorian thought about being animals instead of humans,and at that moment they both changed into huge panthers,the bones in their bodies reforming into a panther like skeletal form as their clothes ripped from their new huge sizes.

Dorian gave Andre a grunt,wanting Andre to follow him as he began running into the trees on all fours,Andre following behind him.

The trees flew pass Andre and Dorian as they bolted through the woods in their panther forms,going speeds neither normal nonshapeshifting humans or animals were capable of.Dorian and Andre stopped as they approached unsuspecting deer in the open grassy field.Watch me get this one,Dorian spoke telepathically to Andre as he crouched,ready to attack the deer.

A huge jet black panther leaped into the open field,catching the deer in it's sharp fangs before Dorian could leap.The panther snapped the deers neck with it's strong jaws,and then glared at Dorian and Andre with gleaming red eyes.

The panthers dark fur nearly matched the night sky,tho the moonlight still gave enough light for things to be seen.Night or day,Andre and Dorian could see clearly either way,because shapeshifters had heightened vision,strength,speed,senses,and healing as well.

The huge black panther headed slowly to Andre and Dorian on all fours,growling faintly at them as they growled back at him,approaching him as well.Andre and Dorian continued to growl at the other panther as they all got close in touchable distance,but then the growls stopped as they all began to lick each other with affection,the other unknown panther licking Andre and Dorian as if they were his cubs.

Andre and Dorian reverted back into their human forms as they stood to their feet again,now standing side by side in their nakedness.The other panther began shifting into his human form as well,now changing into a tall dark brown skinned african american male,resembling Andre in physical appearance,tho he had his own features too.

The man stood to his feet in his nakedness,his eyes on Andre and Dorian.

My boys! The man spoke to Andre and Dorian with excitement in his face,forgetting about the deer he killed that laid not far from his bare feet.Hey pops! Both Andre and Dorian smiled widely at the man,the man who was Deandre,their father.

Dorian you hunt like a pussy! Deandre spoke to Dorian as he embraced both him and Andre in his arms.Whatever pops,i could've had that deer if you wouldn't have stole the motherfucker,Dorian grinned at Deandre.Please little nigga,you just got poor hunting skills,Deandre explained to Dorian with a smirk,his arms still around him and Andre.

Andre,why you aint hunting like ya brother? Deandre questioned Andre with a thin smile.I leave that hunting shit to you and Dorian,i dont see how yall do it? Andre spoke to Deandre with a slight grin.Yea,yea,excuses nigga,Deandre spoke to Andre.

Yall know it's a lot of hunters out there tonight,them niggas know most of us change unwillingly around this time,so the full moon is their hunting season,Deandre explained to Andre and Dorian.Yea,we know,both Andre and Dorian spoke to Deandre.

Hunters were humans who knew about the existence of shapeshifters and everything a part of their supernatural world,tho they kept the existence of shapeshifters secret,just as the shapeshifters themselves did.

Yall two niggas been fucking,i can smell yall scents on each other? Deandre spoke to Andre and Dorian,his face confused.Andre and Dorian gave Deandre guilty facial expressions and then glanced at each other for a second,and then turning their guilty gaze back to Deandre.

Do i sense guilt? Deandre smirked at Andre and Dorian.Pops,Andre uttered,tho his sentence was cut short by Deandre's words.Aint no need in yall explaining anything to me,i kinda knew this would end up happening,i didn't help by giving yall two little niggas baths together when yall was kids,i guess yall keeping it all in the family huh? Deandre spoke to Andre and Dorian,snickering deeply in his deep and immense voice afterwards.

Dorian and Andre began chuckling silently along with Deandre.Another huge panther ran up beside Deandre,and then began changing into it's human form,taking the form of a tall dark skinned man,his skin almost as dark as the night.Oh this my friend Lewis,he cool people,Deandre introduced the tall dark man to Andre and Dorian.

Hey,what's up man? Both Andre and Dorian introduced themselves to Lewis,smiles on their faces.Im good,what's good wit chall? Lewis spoke back to Andre and Dorian,bumping his fists into theirs.

my sons gay too,they swing just like us,Deandre explained to Lewis with a grin.Man yall father told me about yall,but i didn't know yall two dudes was so good looking? Lewis complimented Andre and Dorian.Thank's man,Andre thanked Lewis.Likewise dawg,Dorian spoke to Lewis.

Yall pops told yall about all the hunters that was out tonight,shit is crazy,yall bump into any? Lewis spoke to Andre and Dorian,his eyes watching their faces.Naw,we been just tracking deers and shit,Andre explained to Lewis.

Alright,we about to be out,see yall,Dorian waved at Deandre and Lewis.Peace out,Andre waved at Denadre and lewis as well,turning around,him and Dorian about to head the other way.Wait,let me and Lewis kick it wit chall! Deandre explained to Andre and Dorian before they could run off.Alright,cool,that's what's up,you aint even have to ask pop,you know you welcome man,Andre spoke to Deandre,Dorian agreeing.

Stop checking my sons asses out Lewis,Deandre chuckled softly to Lewis,seeing Lewis's roaming eyes.Naw,i was just looking,Lewis stuttered to Deandre,his face sort of guilty.Let's get out this bitch before some hunters come pass this motherfucker,i aint got time to be clawing a nigga to death,Deandre spoke as he and Andre,Dorian and Lewis all ran in the same direction,shifting into their panther forms all at the same time as they all ran side by side.

Chapter 5

Andre,Dorian,Deandre,and Lewis changed back into their human forms after they reached the house,their nudity even more visible as they entered the lighted house.

Come on,let's hit the showers yall,and have some grown men conversation,Deandre ordered Andre,Dorian and Lewis as they followed him into the master bath.This a big ass house,Lewis spoke to Andre,Dorian and Deandre,as they all soaped themsleves up under the pouring showerheads.Yea,i wanted to keep this baby in the family,that's why i gave it over to my two boys,Deandre explained to Lewis as Lewis listened.True that,Lewis said to Deandre.

I had brought another house not too far from here,imma take you there one of these days,Deandre explained to Lewis,a smile on his face.That's cool wit me,Lewis spoke to Deandre,still soaping himself.

Yall two little dudes got boyfriends? Lewis questioned Andre and Dorian,his eyes on their faces.Shit complicated,Dorian answered Lewis as he looked over at Andre,Andre looking back silently.

So i take that as a no then i guess? Lewis spoke,now rinsing the soap off his muscular body.Shid,yall want me to be yall boyfriend,i can be yall father boyfriend and yalls,yall can keep me all in the family,Lewis joked with Andre and Dorian,a wide grin on his very handsome face.Andre and Dorian began to laugh in response to Lewis as Lewis and Deandre joined them.

Andre and Dorian pulled the same short white towels they used from last time around their waists as they headed out the steamy master bath naked and damp,Deandre and Lewis following behind them,pulling towels around the waists of their naked bodies too.

So yall get a lot of play in here? Lewis questioned Andre and Dorian,a smirk on his face.Hell yea,Dorian smiled at

Lewis,and then at Andre.Can we all kick it upstairs,maybe watch a movie or something? Lewis spoke to Andre,Dorian and Deandre.Yea,that's cool,we can all go to my room,Andre explained to Lewis.

Andre,Dorian,and Deandre and Lewis all headed to Andre's bedroom,where they still lounged around in nothing but the towels they wore around their waists,talking about sex and more sex.

Tell Lewis what chu and ya brother been doing,Deandre smirked at Andre,unable to control his laughter.Pop you putting me on blast huh? Andre smirked back at Deandre with a guilty expression.I had Andre with his mother Natasha when me and her was messing around,and i took Dorian in as my own,now them two niggas fucking,Deandre explained to Lewis,grinning in the process.

Oh damn,so yall literally keeping it in the family huh? Lewis spoke to Andre and Dorian with a slight smirk.Shid,if yall doing shit like that,i bet chall would probably have a foursome in this joint,would yall? Lewis spoke as he leaned back on Andre's bed,and then began stroking himself slowly in a circular motion as Andre,Dorian,and Deandre watched with slight surprise.

Lewis licked his lips smoothly as he jerked himself up and down.Damn dude,warn me next time,Andre spoke to Lewis with a smirk,seeing Lewis stroking away.Yall do it too,yall never jacked off in a group? Lewis spoke to Andre,Dorian and Deandre.Im down,but my sons probably aint with this shit,yall cool wit it? Deandre spoke to Andre and Dorian.It's cool,i know what sex and everything is,Andre explained to Deandre.Shid im in,Dorian spoke.

Fuck man,a father and his sons,this shit is too fucking sexy and hott man,yall got me in here hard as a rock man! Lewis moaned as he continued to stroke his dick.Andre and Dorian began kissing,feeling it was appropriate,seeing that Lewis had already set the mood.

That's what's up,Lewis spoke as he watched Andre and Dorian kiss provocatively,his hands beating his throbbing dick even harder.Can me and yall pops join in on the action? Lewis spoke to Andre and Dorian.Andre let Lewis know he and Dorian's answer as he began jacking

Lewis's hard dick for him,while still kissing Dorian.

Shit,fuck yea! Lewis spoke,his arousal shooting through the roof.Come on pops,you going let cha sons do all the work? Andre spoke to Deandre.It aint a thing,watch yall pops in action,Deandre boasted as he began kissing Lewis,Lewis pushing his tongue into Deandre's mouth,both of them letting their tongues unite as Andre jerked Lewis even harder.

Deandre pulled Lewis's towel to the floor as he began helping Andre jerk Lewis's dick off.Andre got between Lewis's legs as he began sucking and gulping Lewis's dick viciously,his head bobbing and bouncing on Lewis's wet dick as Lewis grunted out in ecstasy,his lips still connected to Deandre's.

Dorian began kissing up and down Andre's back as Andre continued his mouth suction on Lewis.Lewis stood to his feet,and then gently pushed Deandre inbetween his legs with Andre,making both father and son take turns devouring his hard dick.Lewis was in his kinky fantasy bliss,having a father and son,and a brother all in one room to hisself.

Lewis shoved his dick into Deandre's mouth and then shoved it back into Andre's mouth,and then both Andre and Deandre gliding their tongues on each side of Lewis's big hard dick.Dorian began giving Andre a taste of his hard dick as well,pushing Andre's head deeper onto his dick as Deandre began gagging on Lewis's.

Lewis hissed as precum began to slowly escape his dick into Deandre's wet mouth.Dorian gently removed his towel from around his waist as Andre continued to swallow him.Deandre pulled Andre's towel from his waist also,smacking Andre playfully on the ass cheeks afterwards.Deandre stood to his feet,and then dropped his towel from his waist,he and Lewis rubbing and jerking their hard dicks together as Andre's free hand held onto Lewis's strong thigh,Dorian and Lewis now kissing.

Andre,Dorian,Deandre and Lewis were all sandwiched together in a pit of their naked flesh,doing provocative things with each other,tho Deandre never did anything sexual with Andre or Dorian,only smacking them on their asses and rooting them on.Sex scented the room as

Andre,Dorian,Deandre and Lewis continued with their kinky,taboo,and super sexually charged orgy foursome.

Imma about to breed you and ya son nigga,Lewis moaned in Deandre's ear.Andre laid to the bed as Lewis began fucking him hard,Dorian tea bagging Andre in the process as Lewis kissed Deandre,Lewis still grinding himself deep into Andre's cavity until he quickly pulled out,shooting his semen all over Andre's abs,dick and nutsack,letting out a deep moan of pleasure,Deandre's tongue entering his open mouth.

Dorian then shot his semen onto Andre as well,letting out a sigh of release.Andre jerked himself off until he too exploded semen from the tip of his rock hard dick,the semen rolling slowly down his dick head and shaft,and then onto his abs.Deandre and Lewis grunted as they both took turns pounding each other up the ass hard,Deandre eventually cumming heavy and hard,his moans adding to the moans that were already present in the room.

Everyone bumped their fists after they were done with their foursome,their faces exhausted with satisfaction,and their eyes soon closing as they all fell asleep either on the bed or the floor.

Chapter 6

The night passed,and it was now a new day.Andre woke up with Dorian sleeping not too far from him,both of them still naked.Andre felt Dorian's hand grip his arm as he turned towards dorian's open eyes with a thin smile.Deandre and Lewis werent in the room anymore.Andre and

Dorian stood to their feet as they began heading downstairs in the nude.

We out youngsters,Deandre spoke to Andre and Dorian as he kissed both of them on the forehead,and then hugged them,he and Lewis now fully clothed.Deandre and Lewis were wearing expensive slacks and dress shirts,and expensive dress shoes on their feet,clothes that Deandre still had in his old bedroom closet,Andre and Dorian not moving anything out of his old room,feeling that their home was a second home to him.

It was good seeing you pop,Andre spoke to Deandre.Same here dad,Dorian then spoke to Deandre.Yall some cool dudes,but i see yall around,Lewis waved at Andre and Dorian after shaking their hands,and then giving them a quick hug with his shoulders.Deandre and Lewis headed for the front door and then left out,Deandre giving Andre and Dorian one more goodbye wave before fully exiting the house with his male friend Lewis.

Andre and Dorian eyed each other after Deandre and Lewis were gone,and then kissed each other softly on the lips.

Andre and Dorian showered and then got dressed,before heading out to the bayou just a few miles away from their house.Andre and Dorian threw rocks into the water as they spoke silently to each other.Man i cant believe we had a foursome wit our dad dude,Dorian spoke to Andre,still throwing rocks into the water.I know man,shit was wild but fun tho,Andre spoke to Dorian.True,Dorian smiled at Andre.

Man did you ever think me and you would hookup dawg? Dorian

questioned Andre.Man i cant say,i always looked at chu like my homeboy and bro,so when we did our thing,i was kinda shocked,Andre explained to Dorian,the dim sunlight gleaming through the trees onto the water of the bayou.

Man before we had sex dawg i already loved you man,i think that made that shit even better man,Dorian spoke to Andre.I feel you man,i was thinking the exact same thing,Andre explained to Dorian in a soft voice as he threw another rock into the water.Come sit down next to me man,Andre requested of Dorian as he sat to the grass,his knees hunched.

Dorian sat gently next to Andre,his knees hunching as well.Nigga would you ever consider spending eternity with me,i mean,we dont age and shit,we dont get diseases,and we nearly invincible,would you? Andre spoke to Dorian softly.Dawg imma tell you like this,we been raised and living together for like twenty something years,so what's wrong with us spending another twenty something years together or eternity,nothing,Dorian spoke to Andre warmly.

Andre smirked at Dorian,and then pulled his arm around Dorian's shoulder as Dorian pulled his arm around his shoulder,the both of them sitting silently on the grass together as they watched the sparkling water of the bayou,their heads leaning toward each other.

Chapter 7

A month had passed,and it was now a friday afternoon.Andre and Dorian sat on their leather sofa side by side,watching the tv as they joked and played around every now and then,but soon their joking stopped,and their eyes were no longer watching the tv set.Andre and Dorian could hear gunfire,and they could hear low footsteps approaching their house.

Andre headed to the front door,and then quickly opened the door,seeing a man approaching the house slowly,his eyes on Andre and Dorian's faces.

Can we help you man? Andre questioned the man.Hunters,they every fucking where! The man explained to Andre and Dorian as he got closer to the house.A few of my pack members got shot,their wounds are healing,i managed to get away,the man continued to explain to Andre and Dorian.

You two not worried about the hunters? The man questioned Andre and Dorian.Naw,our land is off limits to the hunters,something our father arranged years and years ago,200 years ago to be exact,Andre explained to the scared man.

The two of you are a pure born pack right? The man questioned Andre and Dorian.Yea,we are,Dorian spoke to the man.Cool,so you could handle yourselves just a much as a turned shapeshifter like me could,the man spoke to Dorian and Andre.A man and woman wearing blood drenched clothes walked alongside of the man that spoke with Andre and Dorian.

Spence,Paula! The man spoke in surprise as he turned to the man and woman,hugging them.We killed the hunters before we left,they barely saw it coming,the man Spence explained to the man.Why are you here Blake? The woman Paula questioned the man.I came to warn the two pure borns there about the hunters,Blake pointed to Andre and Dorian.

This is my pack,Blake spoke to Andre and Dorian as he pointed at Spence and Paula.You two should leave,find another part of the woods to stay,that's what we are doing,Paula explained to Andre and Dorian.Naw,we good,Dorian spoke calmly to Paula.My names Blake,we're gone now,you two be careful,Blake spoke to Andre and Dorian,he and his pack departing from Andre and Dorian's sight deep into the woods.

Andre and Dorian headed back into the house,and then shut and locked the door behind them.Andre and Dorian then stripped naked and then headed into the master bath,showering for hours as they laughed and spoke to each other.

You trying do something? Dorian spoke silently to Andre as the raining showerhead poured down on them.That's cool with me,Andre spoke silently back to Dorian.Let me fuck you this time,i aint had no ass in a minute,Dorian spoke to Andre as he bit his lip slightly.Alright,all is fair man,Andre spoke to Dorian as they began kissing and touching each other.

Andre and Dorian headed out the shower,and then pulled short white towels around the waists of their naked bodies,Dorian pulling his arm around Andre's shoulder as they headed down the big marble floored hallway.

Let's go for a run,Dorian spoke to Andre.Like this? Andre questioned Dorian.Yea,aint no use in putting on clothes,we might end up shifting anyway,no use in ripping and fucking up our good clothes bro,Dorian explained to Andre.Alright,Andre spoke back to Dorian.

Andre and Dorian headed out the house wearing nothing but short white towels and shower shoes,no clothes,the warm breeze whisking across their bare skin.Andre and Dorian then bolted into the woods side by side,their strong legs taking them faster and faster through the trees.

Andre and Dorian were moving so fast that they appeared blurry,tho they eventually slowed down,enough to where you were able to see them,tho their bodies were still moving at rapid speed through the woods.Tho Andre and Dorian were moving fast,they could still see every angle,nook and cranny,and the small particles in the air,their eyes reacting like a microscope when needed.

Andre and Dorian stopped once they reached a small secluded field deep in the woods,the dim sunlight shining on the area.

Andre and Dorian turned to each other,and then stared each other down in lust.I can do you right here nigga,Dorian whispered seductively in Andre's ear as they tied their strong arms around each other tightly.So you trying fuck me in the woods huh,i get chu,that's why you got us out here in the middle of nowhere in nothing but towels,easy access huh? Andre smirked at Dorian,Dorian tonguing Andre down in the mouth afterwards,his firm lips then tasting Andre's lips softly.

Dorian grazed his lips across Andre's cheek as they continued to embrace.You want cha bro in you dawg? Dorian questioned Andre in a soft moan of his lips.

Dorian pushed his lips onto Andre's,and then removed them as his ears twitched,he could hear

something,and so did Andre.You hear
that man? Dorian questioned Andre
silently,his eyes glowing red
now.Yea,i do,Andre answered
Dorian,his eyes glowing red now as
well.

Andre and Dorian's bodies tensed up
as they felt someone or something
approach.Andre and Dorian flinched
as they heard guns being loaded and
cocked.The black barrel of a gun
pointed from out the bushes as a
bullet shot from it,aiming directly
towards Andre.Andre's eyes zoomed
in to the approaching bullet as he
dodged it quickly.Another bullet

escaped the barrell of the half hidden gun,the bullet zooming pass Dorian's face,missing him by an inch.

The barrell of the gun moved forward out of the bushes,revealing the rest of the gun,and the man who held onto it.

Hold back Phil,remember,these guys are fast and strong,you know the hunters code! Another man spoke to the gun wielding man as he exited the bushes also.Man look,we aint trying to fight yall today,now please leave me and my brother alone,im warning yall man,Dorian explained calmly to the two men,Andre now standing beside him.

I hate your kind,not only are you and him shapeshifters but your a bunch of fags,Phil spoke to Dorian,disgust on his face.Trevor we should blow these fuckers away now,Phil spoke to the other man beside him.I couldn't agree with you more,Trevor spoke as he and Phil cocked their guns and then began to fire at Dorian and Andre.

Dorian swell into a huge half man and half panther beast as he gently stood protectively in front of Andre,taking full impact of the flying bullets.The bullets bounced from Dorian's thick rhino like skin as he grew even taller,his arms even more muscular than before,and his six pack hardening as his thighs bulged and his claws extended,fine black fur covering his body,his wide and broad chest mostly.

Dorian roared at Phil and Trevor as he approached them,his fangs clinched together and his towel falling from his new big eight feet tall and still growing body.Dorian hovered above Phil and Trevor,his breathing heavy as growls escaped his fangs from the pit of his throat.Dorian swung his right strong long and furry arm at Phil,slapping Phil fifteen feet in the air onto a tree.Trevor lifted the gun that swung around his neck from a gun strap,and then began firing at Dorian,but Dorian still approached him,shaking off the bullets like they were nothing,and then grabbing Trevor by the throat as he picked him up off his feet,choking him with his enhanced strength.

Trevor choked out as Dorian continued to squeeze onto his neck tightly with one hand.Dorian then dropped Trevor from his strong grip,allowing Trevor to get back to his feet.Trevor pulled his hands up in a surrendering way as he quickly backed away from Dorian,and then ran into the bushes,leaving his gun and Phil behind.

Phil stood to his feet again,and then watched Dorian in fear as he followed behind Trevor into the bushes,fleeing Dorian and Andre's sight.

Dorian didn't want to kill Trevor or Phil,he just wanted to scare them,get them away from him and Andre.Dorian you alright bro? Andre spoke to Dorian,tho Dorian didn't answer.Dorian turned towards Andre as he placed his towel back around his naked waist,and then began approaching him in his new beastly man form,his eyes on Andre's face.

Dawg i could've changed like you too,you didn't have to protect me,you know them bullets wouldn't have killed me anyway,they would've hurted,but not kill me,but thank you man,i respect that shit,Andre explained to Dorian as Dorian looked down at him.

Pure born shapeshifters could change not only into a huge overgrown panther,but a huge humanoid panther man beast as well,a beast that had attributes of both animal and man,neatly rolled into one nearly unstoppable being.

Dorian still resembled himself,but with a more extreme beast like appeal.Dorian's big hands gently grazed along Andre's shoulder,his huge size even making Andre appear smaller.You can change back now nigga,Andre smirked at Dorian.

Dorian's hand caressed Andre's face,and then moved down to Andre's pecks,tracing the structure.Dorian threw his towel from his waist as he stared at Andre,his silent growls still hearable.Andre examined Dorian's huge size and naked body,seeing the thin dark fur tracing down from Dorian's chest to Dorian's furry crotch,tho Dorian's penis was still visible,and bigger than before,swinging like a stallions.

Dawg i know you aint trying fuck me why you like that? Andre questioned Dorian.Dorian ignored Andre as he gently turned Andre around.Go easy alright bro,Andre spoke softly to Dorian.Dorian growled as he placed himself into Andre,throwing Andre's towel to the grass.Andre flinched and spasmed as Dorian shoved his penis onto him.Dorian released a high level of pheromones through his pores as he began thrusting,massaging,ramming and making animalistic love to Andre.

Andre was sexually intoxicated by the pheromones Dorian released.Dorian had Andre in doggystyle for hours,until he blew his load.

Chapter 8

The sun was beginning to set,and Andre and Dorian were sleeping quietly next to each other on a tree,their backs against the trees bark,Dorian now back in his human form.

Dorian opened his eyes,and then began kissing on Andre's neck,causing Andre to wake up too.You got the fuck of ya life didn't you Dre? Dorian questioned Andre,using Andre's nickname.Nigga yous a wild dude,Andre smirked at Dorian as he began kissing Dorian back.

Dorian and Andre's kissing became more intense and electrifying as theirs lips met continuously with an impulse that couldn't be controlled.Damn nigga,we got each other like that? Dorian breathed as he and Andre finally untied their lips from each other.I guess so dude,Andre breathed back to Dorian.

A trembling surge flowed through Andre and Dorian as they kissed again.The adrenaline like emotions Andre and Dorian were feeling was mutual,both Andre and Dorian could feel the intensity of it,feeling as if they could complete each others sentences if they wanted,and they did for a second.

We just bonded dude,Dorian spoke silently to Andre.Bonded? Andre spoke.Yea man,bonded,it's another name for it,it's called imprinted,some animals do it all the time,we just imprinted on each other dude,Dorian explained to Andre,knowing what the intense surge he and Andre were feeling was.Yea,i remember pops had told us about something like this a long time ago,Andre spoke to Dorian.

Shapeshifters had humanity and animal instincts,and once Andre and Dorian realized they were in love their animal instincts kicked in,and caused them to imprint on each other.

Come on,let's take our black asses home,Dorian pulled Andre to his feet.Andre and Dorian headed home,but then caught Deandre and Lewis in their sight,Deandre sporting a wide smirk.

My two sons then imprinted,i'll be damned,Deandre smiled at Andre and Deandre as they got closer.Ay pops,ay Lewis,both Andre and Dorian spoke.What's up baby boys,Deandre and Lewis both spoke to Andre and Dorian.How you know we imprinted? Andre questioned Deandre.Yall hearts beating the same patterns,and you my son,so i gotta natural link to you,and i imprinted on Dorian when he was just a baby,but not in the way yall imprinted,i imprinted on Dorian in a fatherly way,the way some adult animals imprint on a cub,so i know him like the back of my hand too,Deandre explained to Andre.

Yall two the third pair in shapeshifter existence to imprint in this century,a gay pair at that,yall know yall going cause some drama,Deandre explained to Andre and Dorian,chuckling deeply afterwards.I ran into this dude name Blake

Dorian,he said he had crossed paths with you and Andre earlier on,but he said at that time he didn't realize you was related to a pack that live near his,until he realized they had the same scent as yours,Deandre spoke carefully to Dorian,meeting Dorian's gaze.

Karina,Deandre spoke as a woman eased up from the shadows,her eyes on Dorian.This ya aunt Karina Dorian,i searched for the pack the dude Blake told me about,Deandre explained to Dorian with a thin smile.

Karina was a short woman,had light skin,a couple of shades lighter than

Dorian's,and thick afrocentric latino mixed hair,Karina could pass for creole,and wore bright ethnic style clothes.

Goodness gracious,you got big,Karina spoke with shock in her face as she approached Dorian slowly,her eyes studying his face intensely.Your mother left the country when she was forced to give you up,some of the pack elders felt that she had so called commited a crime by imprinting on your father,who was a human at the time,shapeshifters were not allowed to be with humans at one point in time,Karina explained softly to Dorian as she caressed his arm.

Your mother and father eventually ran off together,but they came looking for you before they left,but by that time the pack elders had pack members take you off,and nobody knew where,Karina spoke to Dorian,her face apologetic.I went out into the woods searching for you,and i found ya scent,but not chu,but i found you now nephew,Karina smiled at Dorian as Dorian smiled thinly back at her.

Come on,the ceremony about to begin,you too,Karina spoke to dorian and then to Andre,pulling both of them by their arms into the woods as Deandre and Lewis followed behind.

Drop the towels boys,it's a part of the imprinting ceremony,i seen it all before,i've had three husbands over the years,i know what a dangeling is,Karina smirked at Dorian and Andre as they approached two neatly formed lines of shapeshifters in their panther forms.Dorian and Andre smirked at each other as they dropped their towels to the grass from their waists,now standing naked before the other shapeshifters.

Karina led Andre and Dorian halfway inbetween the rows of huge shapeshifter panthers,and then transformed herself into a panther as well,her clothes ripping from her body as she joined the rest of the shapeshifters in line.

Deandre stood at the center of the panther shapeshifter line as Lewis joined the line in panther form.These two young men are my sons,and i love em,i love em more than myself,so im happy to see that they returning that love to not only me,but to each other,Deandre spoke with conviction to the panther crowd,his eyes on Andre and Dorian.Yall two bonded on a physical and emotional level,and who knows what the higher power has planned for us? But i know yall two was brought together,i love yall,Deandre spoke to Andre and Dorian,his eyes watering and glimmering just a bit as he said the words proudly.

When two shapeshifters bond that bond is looked at as a form of marriage or union throughout every pack,so we always celebrate it,just like we doing now,Deandre spoke,and then shifted into his panther form,his clothes ripping and falling from his body.

Damn,so now we official? Dorian spoke silently to Andre.Yea,i guess so,Andre spoke silently to Deandre.Kiss me nigga,Dorian whispered to Andre.Aint got to tell me twice,Andre whispered back to Dorian as they both pressed their lips tightly to each other,embracing in their love,union,and nudity.Deandre began roaring to the sky as Andre and Dorian kissed,the other panthers joining in,roaring along with Deandre as Dorian and Andre continued to lip lock.

Chapter 9

A week had passed,and Andre and Dorian were in bliss,loving bliss,and sexual bliss.

Let's hit the shower,Dorian spoke to Andre as he and Andre kissed passionately on the sofa in shirts and sweat pants.Alright,Andre spoke back to Dorian,giving Dorian one more kiss before they both stood to their feet.

Andre and Dorian peeled their clothes from their bodies and then headed into the master bath naked,twisting on one of the showerheads as they entered.Andre and Dorian shared and stood under a hot raining showerhead together for an hour,and then finally headed back out into the grand hall after they were done with their shower,their bodies nude and slightly damp.

Andre and Dorian pulled short white towels around the waists of their naked bodies as they always did after finishing a hot shower,sliding their feet into shower shoes,and then heading into one of the downstairs bedrooms.

Dorian headed slowly towards Andre,and then pulled his arm around Andre as Andre pulled his arm around him.Andre and Dorian stood lip to lip,chest to chest,muscle to muscle,toned abs to toned abs,towel to towel,thigh to thigh,and knee to knee as they embraced.

Andre began to kiss Dorian softly on the chest,and then worked his lips down further to Dorian's navel as he kneeled to his knees.Dorian began caressing the back of Andre's head with his strong hands as Andre began kissing his inner thigh,causing him to spasm just a bit in response.

Andre then reached his hand underneath Dorian's towel,gripping his fingers around the shaft of Dorian's dick as he began stroking it off slowly,letting Dorian's dick head throb and pulse back and forth in his grip.Dorian's dick got harder as Andre began speeding up with his jerking off session.Andre stuffed the tip of Dorian's huge mushroom shaped penis head into his mouth,engorging on it greedily with gluttony,eager for a taste of Dorian's cum.Dorian moaned out as Andre continued to swallow his dick whole,Dorian feeling the roof and throat of Andre's wet and hot mouth.Andre eased his hand under his own towel as he began jerking himself off while still bouncing his head swiftly back and forth on Dorian's dick,his mouth creating a suction.Suck that nut out nigga! Dorian moaned to Andre in deep pleasure,his face drenched in pure ecstasy of Andre's dick sucking procedure.

Make that shit bust dawg,Dorian pleaded to Andre with a moan.Yea nigga,nut all in my mouth,Andre commanded Dorian as he gulped and swallowed him ferociously in speed and accurate pleasure points,knowing he could cause Dorian to explode at any moment.Andre got even more sloppy and slutty with his dick sucking technique,rolling his tongue around the edge of Dorian's dick head,and then licking the shaft of Dorian's swollen dick as he teased the head again,his tongue tasting the cum hole,and then his mouth swallowing the entire big and thick well endowed rock hard dick again.

Andre kept swallowing Dorian's dick until Dorian's hot flowing thick cum flooded into his mouth from his insanely throbbing dick head,drowning his tongue and mouth.Andre cleaned Dorian's dick head and shaft with his mouth and tongue as Dorian moaned and gasped in good release,Andre then standing to his feet again,his own dick precumming just a tiny bit.

Dorian got to his knees next as he pulled his hands underneath Andre's towel,tasting the precum on Andre's dick head as he licked his lips slowly.Dorian then slapped his face with Andre's hard dick,and then glided it smoothly into his mouth as his head began to move and bounce in rhythm on it.Dorian began jerking his own dick from under his towel,his own cum and the wetness of Andre's mouth still lubricating his dick as he gagged on Andre's.Greedy Gulping sounds filled the room as Dorian devoured Andre's hard dick.Feed me that cum bro,Dorian moaned silently to Andre,begging for Andre's cum down his throat.Andre began tossing Dorian's head back and forth on his dick as he moaned deeply,his dick becoming even more solid and stiff.Dorian then choked and massaged the shaft of Andre's dick as he continued to swallow it.Dorian then slid Andre's dick just halfway out his mouth as Andre's dick began to shoot off thick white cum,Dorian wanting Andre to see the full view of the hot semen entering his mouth.Dorian shoved Andre's ejaculating dick back into his mouth and then began sucking on it again,tasting Andre's cum as his tongue pervertedly licked the shaft and head of Andre's hard and swollen cum covered dick.

Dorian looked up at Andre,and then gave Andre's dick another gulp as Andre's dick shot another round of cum into his mouth,flooding and filling his mouth even more.Dorian then smoothly grazed Andre's cum dripping dick all around his face as Andre continued to bust off loads,giving him a cum facial.

Dorian continued to suck Andre until Andre's dick was clean and empty of cum,and then cleaning his own cheeks with his tongue as he stood back to his feet next to Andre.

Let me fuck that tight ass man,Dorian spoke to Andre.Andre laid himself to the bed next to the window on his back,feeling his dick reloading on semen as Dorian towered over him.Dorian began smoothly massaging he and Andre's dicks together like two big serpents intertwining as they both began to orgasm slightly,but no fully.Dorian pulled Andre's thigh around his waist as he slid himself smoothly into Andre's entrance,causing Andre to gasp out slightly.Dorian then pulled he and Andre's towels from their waists as he went deeper into Andre.

Andre could feel Dorian digging into him with powerful strokes,Dorian's dick moving back and forth into Andre like a power drill.Dorian's dick began hitting the inner walls of

Andre's ass as Andre moaned and jacked off.Andre's head began hitting against the pillow as Dorian plowed deep up into his ass.You want that hot cum in you bro?Dorian moaned to Andre while still thrusting him.Yea nigga,put that nut up in me,Andre spoke to Dorian as he grabbed Dorian's flexing ass.

Dorian began ejaculating into Andre as Andre began to cum all over himself.Dorian then took his dick out of Andre while he was still cumming,squirting his semen all over Andre's naked body as both he and

Andre moaned and breathed in pleasure.

Dorian then laid himself on top of Andre after he and Andre were sexually satisfied,their bodies naked and wet,covered in each others man fluids.

Andre and Dorian loved each other,but were in love as well,their brotherly love evolving into something further and more romantic since the first day they had sex,they were mates now.

Andre and Dorian then fell asleep together,still covered in the intense fornication they had,sleeping in the nude throughout only half the night,waking up a few hours later,fucking again,and then showering all the wild butt naked erotic sex they had from their naked bodies,pulling clean white short and skimpy towels around their naked waists as they headed outside,the warm air of the outdoors swirling and brushing along their practically naked bodies as they stood underneath the dark sky and moon side by side.

The end

www.ingramcontent.com/pod-product-compliance
Lightning Source LLC
Chambersburg PA
CBHW020421290526
45785CB00002B/665